A Call to Protect Our Planet

"World Environment Day"

(05 June 2023)

By: Shehzad Arfan

Table of Contents

Chapter 1

The History of World Environment Day on 5 June

World Environment Day (WED) is celebrated annually on 5 June and is one of the most significant events in the international environmental calendar. This day has been observed since 1974 and is marked by various activities and events worldwide to promote awareness and action for the protection of the environment.

The idea of World Environment Day was proposed at the United Nations Conference on the Human Environment held in Stockholm, Sweden, in 1972. During this conference, delegates from around the world recognized the urgent need for global action to address environmental issues, including pollution, deforestation, and habitat destruction.

On the recommendation of the Conference, the United Nations General Assembly established World Environment Day in 1972, and the first celebration was held two years later in 1974. The theme for the first World Environment Day was "Only One Earth," emphasizing the importance of preserving the planet's limited resources.

Since then, WED has been celebrated annually on 5 June with a different theme every year. Each theme aims to draw attention to a particular environmental issue and encourage individuals, organizations, and governments to take action to address it.

In 1987, the theme of WED was "Environment and Shelter: More Than a Roof," highlighting the importance of adequate housing and the role of the environment in providing it. The following year, in 1988, the theme was "When People Put the Environment First, Development Will Last," emphasizing the importance of sustainable development.

In 1990, WED marked the start of the Earth Summit in Rio de Janeiro, Brazil, which led to the adoption of the United Nations Framework Convention on Climate Change and the Convention on Biological Diversity. The theme for the year was "Children and the Environment," focusing on the importance of educating young people about environmental issues.

In 2002, the theme for WED was "Give Earth a Chance," highlighting the need for conservation and sustainable use of the planet's resources. The following year, in 2003, the theme was "Water: Two Billion People Are Dying for It!" drawing attention to the urgent need to address the global water crisis.

In recent years, the themes of WED have focused on issues such as air pollution, plastic pollution, and biodiversity loss. For example, the theme for 2018 was "Beat Plastic Pollution," encouraging individuals and governments to take action to reduce plastic waste, while the theme for 2021 was "Ecosystem Restoration," highlighting the need to restore degraded ecosystems and protect biodiversity.

In conclusion, World Environment Day has been celebrated annually on 5 June since 1974, with the aim of promoting awareness and action for the protection of the environment. Each year, a different theme is chosen to draw attention to a particular environmental issue and encourage individuals, organizations, and governments to take action to address it. WED serves as a reminder that environmental issues are global and require collective action to be addressed.

Chapter 2

Our Planet, Our Home: The Importance of World Environment Day 2023

The Earth is our home, and it is up to all of us to protect it. World Environment Day, celebrated annually on June 5th, is an important day for raising awareness about environmental issues and promoting action to protect our planet.

The theme for World Environment Day 2023 is "Ecosystem Restoration," highlighting the urgent need to repair and restore damaged ecosystems. This theme underscores the fact that the health of our planet is intimately tied to the health of its ecosystems, and that we must take action to protect and restore them.

Ecosystems provide us with essential services such as clean air and water, food, and raw materials for industry. They also play a critical role in regulating the Earth's climate, absorbing carbon dioxide and other greenhouse gases from the atmosphere. However, ecosystems are under threat from a range of human activities such as deforestation, pollution, and climate change.

World Environment Day 2023 presents an opportunity to reflect on the importance of our planet and the role that we all play in protecting it. We must recognize that our actions have consequences, and that we have a responsibility to act in ways that minimize harm to the environment.

One of the most important ways that we can protect the environment is by reducing our carbon footprint. Carbon dioxide emissions are a major contributor to climate change, which is one of the most pressing environmental issues facing the world today. We can reduce our carbon footprint by using energy-efficient appliances, driving less, and eating a more plant-based diet.

Another important way that we can protect the environment is by reducing waste. This includes reducing the use of single-use plastics, recycling, and composting. By reducing waste, we can reduce the amount of materials that end up in landfills, which can contribute to pollution and greenhouse gas emissions.

Finally, we must recognize that environmental issues are complex and multifaceted. They require solutions that are holistic, integrated, and collaborative. This means that individuals, communities, governments, and businesses must all work together to address environmental issues.

In conclusion, our planet is our home, and it is up to all of us to protect it. World Environment Day 2023 is an important opportunity to reflect on the importance of our planet and the role that we all play in protecting it. By taking action to reduce our carbon footprint, reduce waste, and work collaboratively, we can ensure that our planet remains a healthy and vibrant home for generations to come.

Chapter 3

Taking Action for a Sustainable Future: Celebrating World Environment Day 2023

World Environment Day 2023 is a time for celebrating our planet and taking action towards a sustainable future. The theme for this year's celebration is "Ecosystem Restoration," which highlights the importance of repairing and restoring damaged ecosystems.

Sustainability is the key to achieving a better future for all. It requires us to live in harmony with our planet and to meet the needs of the present without compromising the ability of future generations to meet their own needs. This means adopting a holistic approach that considers social, economic, and environmental factors.

Taking action for a sustainable future involves making changes at every level, from individual actions to global policy decisions. Some actions that individuals can take include reducing energy consumption, using public transportation, and supporting local businesses. Governments can take action by implementing policies that encourage sustainability, such as promoting renewable energy and reducing greenhouse gas emissions.

Businesses also have a role to play in achieving a sustainable future. They can do this by adopting sustainable practices in their operations, such as reducing waste and using sustainable materials. They can also invest in renewable energy and support sustainable supply chains.

One important way that we can take action for a sustainable future is by promoting environmental education. By educating people about environmental issues, we can raise awareness and inspire action. This can be done through schools, community programs, and media campaigns.

In addition to taking action at the individual, government, and business levels, we can also work together to achieve a sustainable future. This means collaborating across sectors and borders to share knowledge and resources, and to work towards common goals.

In conclusion, World Environment Day 2023 is a time for celebrating our planet and taking action towards a sustainable future. By adopting a holistic approach that considers social, economic, and environmental factors, and by taking action at every level, from individual actions to global policy decisions, we can work towards a better future for all. By promoting environmental education and collaborating across sectors and borders, we can ensure that our actions are sustainable and have a lasting impact.

Chapter 4

Biodiversity and Ecosystem Restoration: The Focus of World Environment Day 2023

Biodiversity is the foundation of healthy ecosystems, and healthy ecosystems are essential for the survival of all species, including humans. Unfortunately, human activities such as deforestation, pollution, and climate change are threatening biodiversity and the ecosystems that support it. World Environment Day 2023 focuses on the importance of ecosystem restoration and the role that biodiversity plays in achieving it.

Biodiversity refers to the variety of life on Earth, including the diversity of species, genes, and ecosystems. Ecosystems are the complex interactions between living organisms and their environment, including their physical surroundings such as soil, water, and air. Healthy ecosystems are essential for human well-being, providing services such as food, clean water, and medicine.

Ecosystem restoration involves repairing and restoring damaged ecosystems, which can include activities such as reforestation, wetland restoration, and coral reef restoration. By restoring ecosystems, we can help to reverse the negative effects of human activities and promote biodiversity.

Biodiversity and ecosystem restoration are closely linked, as healthy ecosystems are necessary for the survival of a wide range of species. However, biodiversity loss and ecosystem degradation are occurring at an alarming rate. It is estimated that up to one million species are at risk of extinction, largely due to human activities.

Restoring ecosystems can help to promote biodiversity by providing habitat for a range of species. This, in turn, can help to stabilize ecosystems, making them more resilient to climate change and other environmental stressors. Restoring ecosystems can also help to provide ecosystem services such as carbon sequestration and water purification.

World Environment Day 2023 provides an opportunity to reflect on the importance of biodiversity and ecosystem restoration, and to take action towards protecting them. This can involve individual actions such as reducing waste and supporting sustainable agriculture, as well as collective actions such as supporting conservation efforts and advocating for policy change.

In conclusion, biodiversity and ecosystem restoration are essential for the survival of all species, including humans. World Environment Day 2023 focuses on the importance of restoring damaged ecosystems and promoting biodiversity. By taking action to protect and restore ecosystems, we can help to ensure a sustainable future for all.

Chapter 5

From Awareness to Action: Mobilizing for World Environment Day 2023

Awareness is the first step towards taking action for the environment, but it is not enough on its own. World Environment Day 2023 is a time for mobilizing individuals, communities, and organizations to take action towards a sustainable future. This involves moving beyond awareness-raising to mobilizing for action.

Mobilizing for action requires a shift in mindset from passive awareness to active engagement. This means taking responsibility for our actions and recognizing the impact that they have on the environment. It also means recognizing that we have the power to make a difference and taking action to do so.

One important way to mobilize for World Environment Day 2023 is through community action. This can involve organizing events such as clean-up campaigns, tree planting initiatives, and educational workshops. By working together as a community, we can have a greater impact and inspire others to take action.

Another way to mobilize for action is through policy change. Governments can play a key role in promoting sustainability by implementing policies that encourage renewable energy, reduce greenhouse gas emissions, and protect natural resources. By advocating for policy change, individuals and organizations can help to create a more sustainable future for all.

Businesses also have a role to play in mobilizing for World Environment Day 2023. They can do this by adopting sustainable practices in their operations, such as reducing waste and using sustainable materials. They can also invest in renewable energy and support sustainable supply chains. By doing so, businesses can help to drive the transition towards a more sustainable economy.

Finally, mobilizing for action requires a continued commitment to sustainability beyond World Environment Day 2023. This means making sustainable choices in our daily lives, advocating for policy change, and supporting businesses that prioritize sustainability.

In conclusion, World Environment Day 2023 is a time for moving beyond awareness-raising to mobilizing for action. By taking responsibility for our actions, working together as a community, advocating for policy change, and prioritizing sustainability in our daily lives, we can create a more sustainable future for all. It is up to each and every one of us to make a difference and take action towards a more sustainable future.

Chapter 6

Greening Cities and Communities: Local Solutions for Global Problems on World Environment Day 2023

Cities are at the forefront of environmental challenges such as air pollution, waste management, and climate change. However, they also hold the key to solutions for these problems. World Environment Day 2023 focuses on greening cities and communities, highlighting the important role that local solutions can play in addressing global environmental challenges.

Greening cities and communities involves implementing sustainable practices such as green infrastructure, renewable energy, and sustainable transportation. These practices can help to reduce carbon emissions, improve air and water quality, and promote a healthier, more livable environment for residents.

One example of greening cities is the implementation of green infrastructure such as parks, green roofs, and urban forests. These green spaces can help to mitigate the effects of climate change by reducing the urban heat island effect and absorbing carbon dioxide from the atmosphere. They also provide important habitat for biodiversity and promote physical and mental health for residents.

Another example of greening cities is the use of renewable energy such as solar and wind power. By transitioning to renewable energy, cities can reduce their carbon footprint and promote a more sustainable energy system. This can also create jobs and stimulate economic growth.

Sustainable transportation is another important aspect of greening cities and communities. This can involve promoting walking and biking, improving public transportation, and encouraging the use of electric vehicles. By reducing the use of fossil fuels in transportation, cities can reduce air pollution and improve public health.

Greening cities and communities require a collaborative effort between local governments, businesses, and residents. By working together, cities can create a more sustainable and livable environment for all. This can also serve as a model for other cities around the world to follow.

In conclusion, World Environment Day 2023 focuses on the importance of greening cities and communities. By implementing sustainable practices such as green infrastructure, renewable energy, and sustainable transportation, cities can address global environmental challenges such as climate change and improve the quality of life for residents. It is up to all of us to take action towards a more sustainable future for our cities and communities.

Chapter 7

Business and the Environment: Creating a More Sustainable Future on World Environment Day 2023

Businesses have a significant impact on the environment, from their supply chains to their operations and products. However, they also have the potential to play a critical role in creating a more sustainable future. World Environment Day 2023 highlights the importance of businesses in addressing environmental challenges and promoting sustainability.

One important way that businesses can contribute to sustainability is by adopting sustainable practices in their operations. This can involve reducing waste, using renewable energy, and promoting sustainable sourcing of materials. By adopting sustainable practices, businesses can reduce their environmental impact and promote a more sustainable economy.

Another way that businesses can contribute to sustainability is by developing sustainable products and services. This can involve incorporating environmentally friendly materials, promoting circular economy practices, and designing products with a longer lifespan. By developing sustainable products and services, businesses can help to shift consumer behavior towards more sustainable choices.

Businesses can also contribute to sustainability through corporate social responsibility (CSR) initiatives. This can involve supporting community projects such as tree planting initiatives, sponsoring environmental education programs, and supporting conservation efforts. By engaging in CSR initiatives, businesses can demonstrate their commitment to sustainability and contribute to positive social and environmental impacts.

Finally, businesses can contribute to sustainability through collaboration and innovation. By working together with other businesses, governments, and civil society, businesses can develop innovative solutions to environmental challenges. This can involve sharing best practices, investing in research and development, and collaborating on sustainability initiatives.

In conclusion, businesses have a critical role to play in creating a more sustainable future. By adopting sustainable practices in their operations, developing sustainable products and services, engaging in CSR initiatives, and collaborating with others, businesses can help to address environmental challenges and promote sustainability. World Environment Day 2023 is a reminder of the important role that businesses play in creating a more sustainable future, and an opportunity for businesses to take action towards a more sustainable economy.

Chapter 8

Youth Engagement for a Greener Future: Inspiring Change on World Environment Day 2023

Young people are the future leaders and caretakers of the planet. As such, they have an important role to play in shaping a greener, more sustainable future. World Environment Day 2023 focuses on youth engagement and the importance of inspiring change among the next generation of environmental leaders.

Youth engagement can take many forms, from environmental education and awareness-raising to youth-led initiatives and advocacy. By engaging young people in environmental issues, we can empower them to take action and make a positive impact on the planet.

One important way to engage youth in environmental issues is through education. This can involve incorporating environmental topics into school curricula, providing opportunities for outdoor education and experiential learning, and promoting environmental education programs through youth organizations. By providing young people with the knowledge and skills to understand environmental issues, we can inspire them to take action and become environmental leaders in their communities.

Youth-led initiatives and advocacy are another important way to engage young people in environmental issues. This can involve youth-led campaigns to promote sustainable practices, such as reducing plastic waste or promoting sustainable transportation. Youth can also be involved in advocacy efforts to promote environmental policies and raise awareness of environmental issues among policymakers and the general public.

Finally, engaging youth in environmental issues requires creating spaces for youth to voice their opinions and ideas. This can involve creating youth-led organizations and forums, providing opportunities for youth to participate in decision-making processes, and creating safe and inclusive spaces for youth to engage in environmental discussions.

In conclusion, youth engagement is crucial for creating a greener, more sustainable future. By providing young people with the knowledge, skills, and opportunities to engage in environmental issues, we can inspire them to take action and become environmental leaders in their communities. World Environment Day 2023 highlights the importance of youth engagement in environmental issues and provides an opportunity for young people to make a positive impact on the planet.

Chapter 9

Innovations for Sustainability: Showcasing Solutions on World Environment Day 2023

Innovation is critical for achieving sustainability, as it enables us to develop new solutions to environmental challenges and promote a more sustainable future. World Environment Day 2023 highlights the importance of innovation in sustainability and showcases the latest innovations in environmental technology, design, and policy.

Innovations for sustainability can take many forms, from new technologies and materials to innovative policies and business models. By showcasing these innovations, we can inspire others to adopt more sustainable practices and accelerate progress towards a more sustainable future.

One important area of innovation for sustainability is in renewable energy technologies. This can involve developing new and more efficient solar, wind, and hydro power technologies, as well as energy storage solutions. By promoting the use of renewable energy, we can reduce greenhouse gas emissions and promote a more sustainable energy system.

Another area of innovation for sustainability is in sustainable materials and manufacturing processes. This can involve developing new materials that are more environmentally friendly, such as bioplastics or recycled materials. It can also involve developing more sustainable manufacturing processes, such as 3D printing or circular economy practices. By adopting sustainable materials and manufacturing processes, we can reduce waste and promote a more sustainable economy.

Innovative policies and business models are also critical for achieving sustainability. This can involve developing new regulations and incentives to promote sustainability, such as carbon pricing or sustainable procurement policies. It can also involve developing new business models that prioritize sustainability, such as sharing economy platforms or circular economy business models. By promoting innovative policies and business models, we can create a more sustainable economy and promote positive environmental and social impacts.

In conclusion, innovation is critical for achieving sustainability and promoting a more sustainable future. World Environment Day 2023 showcases the latest innovations in environmental technology, design, and policy and highlights the importance of innovation in sustainability. By showcasing these solutions and inspiring others to adopt more sustainable practices, we can accelerate progress towards a more sustainable future.

Chapter 10

Building a Resilient Planet: Preparing for the Future on World Environment Day 2023

As the impacts of climate change become increasingly severe, it is more important than ever to build a resilient planet that can withstand and adapt to these changes. World Environment Day 2023 focuses on the importance of building resilience and preparing for the future, in order to protect the planet and the people who depend on it.

Building a resilient planet involves a wide range of strategies and approaches, from improving infrastructure and disaster preparedness to promoting biodiversity conservation and sustainable land use. By adopting these strategies, we can reduce the impacts of climate change and protect the planet and its inhabitants.

One important strategy for building a resilient planet is to improve infrastructure and disaster preparedness. This can involve investing in infrastructure that is designed to withstand the impacts of climate change, such as sea level rise and extreme weather events. It can also involve developing disaster preparedness plans and response mechanisms, to ensure that communities are prepared for and able to respond to disasters.

Another strategy for building a resilient planet is to promote biodiversity conservation and sustainable land use. This can involve protecting and restoring natural ecosystems, such as forests and wetlands, which can help to regulate the climate and provide important ecosystem services. It can also involve promoting sustainable land use practices, such as agroforestry and regenerative agriculture, which can help to build soil health and promote biodiversity.

Finally, building a resilient planet requires promoting social and economic resilience. This can involve promoting equitable access to resources and opportunities, as well as developing social safety nets and other mechanisms to protect vulnerable populations. It can also involve promoting sustainable economic practices, such as the circular economy and green jobs, which can help to build economic resilience and reduce vulnerability to climate change.

In conclusion, building a resilient planet is critical for preparing for the future and protecting the planet and its inhabitants. World Environment Day 2023 focuses on the importance of building resilience and promoting strategies and approaches that can help us to adapt to the impacts of climate change. By adopting these strategies, we can build a more resilient and sustainable future for all.

Chapter 11

Towards a Net-Zero Future: Accelerating Climate Action on World Environment Day 2023

The impacts of climate change are becoming increasingly severe, and urgent action is needed to address this global crisis. World Environment Day 2023 focuses on accelerating climate action and working towards a net-zero future, in order to mitigate the impacts of climate change and protect the planet and its inhabitants.

A net-zero future involves reducing greenhouse gas emissions to the point where any remaining emissions are balanced by the removal of an equivalent amount of greenhouse gases from the atmosphere. This requires a significant reduction in greenhouse gas emissions, as well as the implementation of strategies and approaches to remove carbon from the atmosphere.

One important strategy for accelerating climate action is to transition to renewable energy sources. This involves reducing the use of fossil fuels and increasing the use of renewable energy sources such as solar, wind, and hydropower. It also involves promoting energy efficiency and conservation, in order to reduce the overall demand for energy.

Another strategy for accelerating climate action is to promote sustainable transportation. This can involve promoting the use of electric vehicles, improving public transportation systems, and encouraging active transportation such as cycling and walking. By reducing emissions from the transportation sector, we can make significant progress towards a net-zero future.

In addition to reducing emissions, it is also important to remove carbon from the atmosphere in order to achieve a net-zero future. This can involve strategies such as reforestation and afforestation, which involve planting trees and increasing forest cover to absorb carbon from the atmosphere. It can also involve the development of carbon capture and storage technologies, which capture carbon dioxide from industrial processes and store it in underground geological formations.

Finally, accelerating climate action requires a collaborative effort from governments, businesses, and individuals. This can involve setting ambitious targets and implementing policies to reduce emissions, as well as promoting innovation and technology development to accelerate the transition to a net-zero future. It also involves promoting awareness and education on the importance of climate action and the impacts of climate change.

In conclusion, accelerating climate action and working towards a net-zero future is critical for addressing the global climate crisis. World Environment Day 2023 focuses on the importance of accelerating climate action and promoting strategies and approaches that can help us to achieve a net-zero future. By adopting these strategies, we can mitigate the impacts of climate change and protect the planet and its inhabitants for generations to come.

Messages

Dear Youngsters,

On this World Environment Day, I encourage you to take action towards a greener and more sustainable future. The choices you make today can have a significant impact on the health of our planet tomorrow. Whether it's reducing your plastic use, planting trees, or advocating for environmental policies, every action count. Your voices and actions can inspire others to join in the movement towards a healthier and more sustainable planet. So, let's work together to make a positive difference for our planet and future generations. Happy World Environment Day!

www.ingramcontent.com/pod-product-compliance
Lightning Source LLC
Chambersburg PA
CBHW051901250726
48659CB00006B/2339